High Wire

High Wire

ADRIAN CAESAR

PANDANUS BOOKS
Research School of Pacific and Asian Studies
THE AUSTRALIAN NATIONAL UNIVERSITY

Cover: *Balancing Act*, watercolour by Romola Templeman

Typeset in Weiss 11pt on 15pt and printed by CanPrint Communications

National Library of Australia Cataloguing-in-Publication entry

Caesar, Adrian, 1955–.
    High wire.

    ISBN 1 74076 178 2.

    I. Title.

A821.3

Published by Pandanus Books, Research School of Pacific and Asian Studies,
The Australian National University, Canberra ACT 0200 Australia

A Sullivan's Creek Publication

Pandanus Books are distributed by UNIREPS, University of New South Wales,
Sydney NSW 2052 Telephone 02 9664 0999 Fax 02 9664 5420

Production: Ian Templeman, Justine Molony and Emily Brissenden

For Claire

Acknowledgements

Some of these poems have appeared previously in the following publications: *Muse, Canberra Times, Westerly, Hobo, Ulitarra, Conversations*.

I am grateful to Bruce Bennett for his editorial suggestions, and would like to thank Ian Templeman and Justine Molony for their commitment to this project.

Contents

Cut Flowers

You have pruned the heads
from the African Marigolds
and floated them in soup bowls
round the house, such orange,
princes of light and dying colour,
they keep surprising the eye
like cluster bombs of some exotic fruit,
or fast food with a catchy title
scattered for nibbling comfort.

Their severed lives make us smile
as if we have gulped sunshine
and forgotten that soon the light goes out.

Re-Cycler

Abendstille überalle ...
The words come back to me
under southern skies
from another hemisphere
twenty years ago at least
my first lover teaching me
the foreign language of rapture
from the farmhouse loft
through the skylight we watched
the wheeling stars.
Du bis mis liebs,
I was taught to whisper
holding your gluhwein warmth
just enough exotic to take me
away from the northern streets
of childhood and adolescence
towards your Swiss mountains
an alpine flowering.

Now it all comes back to me
with the ache of a love song
on a Sunday evening,
wheeling out the week's detritus
the empty bottles of daily comfort,
the no-song of quotidian
middle age, and I stopped
for a moment to wonder
where you've gone and how
your children are and what has
happened to the years I remember
the rain on train windows
tears of our parting, my faithlessness
and stop to wish for a moment
that somewhere you are singing
Abendstille überalle
and that in the darkness pricks
of light still dance and someone
mouths *du bis mis liebs, Mädeli.*

The bins are empty for another week.
I close the door on romance and the past.
'Have you done with the garbage?'
I hear my wife, unknowing, ask,
smiling, 'It's time we were in bed.'

Night Sailing

When I was a child I made the bed
a rocking boat that would sail
through the night, and I so rapt
became a traveller to a place
where all was safe beyond the
clasp of fear's embrace.

But then as now the spell of sleep
was broken by insomnia
the shadow waves of wind tossed trees
stormed about my battered hull
and I was threatened by the ink
of death's commanding signature.

Daylight meant calm seas and green
relief to that young boy
but now by day or night the sailing
isn't plain. I dream or wake
to strange deeps of middle age
I don't know how to navigate.

Here there is no magic,
to dream of romance means
you're sadly immature
and hoping to be safe, the years
bring further fear not sapience:
the ship adrift on a dead lee shore.

And now it seems too late
to learn the mariner's skills
of binding knot and cunning steerage,
the grizzled wisdom that leads
to the Master's or the Pilot's ticket,
a store of moral stories.

The knowledge is missing;
there's no manual for deliverance:
the next port looks terminal.
My only plan to steady and trim,
plot a course as long as I can,
keep from capsize, sink or swim.

In Dublin, 1999

After the terrible intimacy
of breakfast with a stranger
in a boarding house of grief
I read the streets of this writer's city
noting the miserable distance
between Crazy Jane romance
and the beggars who've pissed themselves
their bent and crippled heads
mouthing prayerful imprecations
by the shops selling Celtic souvenirs.

What, I wonder, did I expect?
certainly not the landlady with her
'fucken' dis' and 'fucken' dat'
her talk of the price of real estate
and the latest single by The Corrs,
or the hairdresser from Wexford
with whom I shared the agony
of cornflake crunching silences
following the chastity of single beds.
There was a romance in my head.

It must have been some dark colleen
who'd strayed from a lyric by Yeats
I wanted to meet at the end of the street
where only the destitute fiddler reaped
a coin or two from the chic elite.
'If it weren't for the t'ieves and the t'uggery
sure it'd be a beautiful place,'
said the taxi driver transporting me
to the Municipal Gallery the longest way.
'It's the drugs that do it now.'

Somewhere between the cyber-cafe
and the drunks roaring tunes in the pub
I heard 'Romantic Ireland's dead and gone';
faery, ghost, priest and bead have made
the Ballykissangel of TV dreams,
marketing and tourism provide the creed;
there are many genuflections
in the green and global village of greed.
But still I was seduced: the *craic* was good,
and signs of promise: Guiness is Good For You!

Paris Sponge

(For Bruce and Trish)

In the café La Madeleine du Proust
everything is precious as it should be.
We, the only customers on a moody afternoon,
decide on tea, share cakes, two between four
(the unnecessary sweet confection)
earning the disdain of *les homosexuels*
who perform an expensive ballet;
every task is mime or gesture
for maximum proprietorial effect,
washing dishes, laying plates, preparation
of coffee we are led to understand
is work of the highest order, an art form
waiting to be discovered, while we
the philistines scoured the walls
their black and whites of Sartre, Gide
and Hemingway, *les immortels*,
until the madeleines arrived,
a mere taste, should make the word
death disappear, Proust says, or snap
open the synaptic paths of memory,

but nothing happened, not even a wistful
image of Maddy, my first beloved,
sugar and butter not powerful enough
to conjure that dark girl delighting
to shock with her dangerous expletive.
No, we were left, polite ironical,
four friends savouring time together,
practising the demotic craft of conversation,
cultivating a casual *sang froid*,
knowing the moment won't come back
however hard we try, and is the more
precious for that, as the dark angel beckons
instinct in each sip and bite.

Summer Evening: Glenelg

We walk between the funfare and the sea
the night and the white sand stretch away
into the dark while a thousand gaudy bulbs
bloom to the hurdy gurdy, and febrile shrieks
pursue the clatter of mad trams as they dive
and swoop along eccentric scaffolding.

We'd been rehearsing roles and what remains
beyond their fragile gesture and the play
of our appointed parts: mother, father
policeman, friend, what's left
when the script is stripped away?
Who can we improvise, extempore?

In alleys of crude invention we see
gaping mouths swivel in the glare
and miniature rifles pop their parables
of ambitious violence; *You too can be a winner!*
inviting us to join the toy-town carnival
march to the tune of their competition.

From soft targets to dodgem cars we witness
the bang and crash of brute collision
try the ordinary swings and roundabouts
everywhere encounter the glitz and blitz
the powerful parade of relationship:
save or spend: the spruiker still insists.

Having tasted this gamut of fun and fare
we wander again to the espalanade
and walk towards the dark and stars
where the gentle lap of solitary tides
become a music quite beyond
the fume and fret of community event.

There, a solitary gull swerves,
its wings plated silver by starlight
a momentary ornament
to the idea of individual grace,
a quietness apart, the self pursuing
the artful flight of its own arc.

Beyond the masks of chatter,
when clever lines no longer work
and every gesture has the hollow force
of actors coining cheap devotions,
we make our way between the funfare and the sea
wondering who and what and how to be.

Black-Marks: An Antarctic Notebook

I

It's as if in speaking
too much to himself
he has lost his voice
and become a numb silence

the blank page is Antarctica
and he afraid of the cold
the lonely trek which leaves
no foot print, but white-out

hears only the echoes
of dead ambitions
ghosting across icesheets
and the sound of money

talking loans, percentages
the taxing future
will the explorations
yield a profit

the interest of politicians
can you sell the story
to whom might you speak
with faith and trust?

Here is the journey or refusal
of the journey
to find another language
invent a hundred words for snow

which might record
how long it takes for poetry
to die within a man
who has lost himself

and is trudging forward
knowing how little will change
whether he howls to the wilderness
or not if no one hears.

II

In the white
to keep going despite
a sense of futility
each plodding step
a word upon word
whispering in the crooked steps
of the great
a mantra of black marks:
'travelling hopefully
is better than arrival'
'the value of labour
is greater than lassitude', etc.
Did they really believe?
Can we learn from this?

Some hope for fame
and pay with their lives;
some hope for wealth
and find their lives paid-out;
some hope to do good
and crucify with kindness;
some hope for power
and lead to the grave.
All of them in their way
set goals for themselves,
athletes of splendid wishes
spend midnight time
in dark self-persuasion
I am: my works are good.

Every night
I build my cairn
word upon word
a small show against
faithlessness
with no desire to revisit
flags or empire
position and fame —
those silly foolings in the frost —
there is only this
determined movement
in a silent space
across the blank desert
dreaming of a better place.

III

It is, we know, a great escape
this plunging into white
though art is still intangible
as the barely realised South Pole.
People have died making tracks
though the delirious pen,
charting such defeat has tended
towards the plotting of heroes.
I am not heroic.
But I long for this journey
the uncharted page
where there are no taxes
and the space lies free
of money, power and managers.
Of course you'll say
what's the use? — they said
the same to Scott — he replied
'Science,' though he fibbed
he knew he was walking
into poetry, drama, romance
sucking on opium he made love
to his diary the final devotion

to be sold to a waiting nation
fixing his legend in a fine syntax.
Did he know as he wrote
they'd all be listening
or was it more a making
of himself and his motto
'Ready, Aye Ready'.
I hope, but don't believe
such purity. Legends bore me.
But if you are not there,
(who are you?)
reading on the other side
of this journey
does that mean I might as well
whisper to myself
in rapt self-persuasion
this is how to confer meaning
pretend death has no fear for me,
there it waits beckoning,
the greatest escape of them all
am I making myself
ready, aye ready, to die?

IV

What does it mean
to lose heart
in this white wilderness —
a paper grief
of endless blank sheets
an absence of the beloved
a numb silence
speech frozen
by the enormous effort
of belief, the knowledge
that crowds are now
attending colourful
picture shows
Hollywood peddling
hot stars
truth and justice
to the globe,
while the wars unfold
Christ and civilisation
rammed home
via bomb and bullet

democracy a strongarm
lawless imposition
winning hearts and minds
WHAMO!
while poetry is found
in Pop and Rock and Folk
see the rapt faces
warmed by concerts
in wealthy cities,
as the muse lies
by the fireside
in the suburbs
watching reality TV.
How to go on?
Put one word
in front of another?
Nobody likes the cold
but how to come in
without suffocating
in the heat
at the global hearth?

V

Perhaps we're all trudging
across the snow plain
towards death but somehow
become used to the monotony
let the knowledge of cold
lock further endeavours in.
It is, we sigh to ourselves,
enough to survive.
We will proceed
with our horizons contracting
every day and accept
the daily diminishment
of what might be said
by this pen pushing on
the interminable march.
We become comfortable
with the limitations of landscape
its rigours usual.
Nothing to be done
to change the map that rules
our waking course.

Then, consider this:
treading the edge of language
the snow bridge breaks
an unexpected fissure
plunges you towards oblivion
but the sledge which carries
your world — food, a book or two
letters from the beloved —
stops and you're left
revolving, harnessed to exhausted
silence. Two choices.
Cut the rope and finish —
no more struggle, who would care?
The other: to find
new knotted words
conjure a ropy trick
make a ladder to seek
further articulation
say, look how
I dared the crevasse
in the face of oblivion
survived to tell another tale,
treading the edge again.

VI

You can lose your voice
striving to be heard
across white miles of silence.

Words echo through the skull
like tangled traps and harness
from which you cannot free

a straight and guiding line.
And you can imagine
in this blank impasse

another medium might do the trick.
Perhaps there are others waiting,
unseen, to receive messages

across the icy wastes huddled
by their wireless hoping for
the crackle of life, the codes

of tip-tap dancing, that speak
of salvation from the drear
with words beyond imagining

like love or home.

Josie's Monologue

People who don't know him
might say he deserved it —
I mean the booze and smokes
he was overweight
had no time for puritans
said he was so steeped in sin
there was no chance of redemption.
No matter what he did
he had a one-way ticket to hell.
To look at him latterly,
balding, with a beer gut
hanging over denim jeans,
before his heart stopped,
people would think he was
a blue singlet type of bloke
good for a yarn in the pub
footy and a bet on the nags
on Saturdays. Well yeah,
he was good for all of that.
But he read his Shakespeare
painted his paintings
grew tomatoes by the kilo.
I can still remember the scent
on his broad stubby fingers
the astringent disinfectant smell
of tomato vines, as he placed his hand

against my cheek, and said goodnight.
How can you say the war undid him?
It was his idea of how to be a man
like his father, his father's father before him.
They'd done their bit, wore their medals,
had their fabled stories
which made it all sound grand.
He wouldn't tell me anything.
I used to think it was my fault.
He wanted a boy, not me, a useless girl.
But that's not what he said before he died,
giving me the signet ring, a souvenir
passed between generations of battle
Pozieres, El Alamein, Vietnam.
No, his last gift was this:
try not to destroy too much;
learn how to grow
and taste the apples of love.

The Reluctant Digger

'I'll make a gardener of you yet,' you say
and I, grinning at the improbability;
those English grounds of my childhood
were definitions of restraint,
the pristine bed a sign of ordered boredom,
the shaved lawn dressed to perfection
was not for ragamuffin footballers,
scent and symmetry and tidiness were all
energy contained and impulse tamed.

But here at least we still call it a yard
and though surrounded by trim acres
of politeness it's still possible to cultivate
a determined chaos, an abundance
where we play at educated peasantry
our spinach flanked by roses, spuds
punctuate the nodding blooms, and
capsicum, chilli, aubergines
set their modern art against the fast

McTuckey culture, the fashionable screens,
and encourage this subversive pledge
to try to learn slow-growing virtues,
how the mystery unfolds only if the ground's
prepared with care, and clay is countered
space, light, and water not taken for granted
a useless proliferation of weed won't do:
there is a point to this traditional labour
foot to the spade's edge, though my back aches.

Three Vegetables

I

Capsicum dangle from stalks
their glossy skins like plastic
make me think of novelties
or playthings for children, their squareness
not quite square, their different sizes
might be a puzzle,
they can never be bells
tho' their deep hollow knock
might aspire to drum;
they are unruly sculptures
I'd like to build on some huge scale
and droop in the halls of power
to amaze and confound the suits in grey
who'd bang their heads against such
vegetable strength, such lively
sweet and sour and coloured fun.

II

They don't care how sexy they are
the pendulous purple-black fruit
shining as if oiled breasts
inviting the cupped hand,
but if you prefer the garden chaste
think of them as ornaments
shaped for an Easter mourning,
the dark eggs shining with promise
offering their flesh to our desire
they reward our hunger with ebony
reminders of death; as if we're made
to kill and taste all that might be called
God/Goddess.

III

A miniature phallus or kittens' tails
glossed green or red, go and stop, the chilli's
neat paradox reverses our
cultivated expectations.
The hot invitation offered by green
promises curry for indulgent pleasures,
care is needed here, but the honest
red, signalling danger, always threatens
that we might have to pay later
given our lust for taste, taste for lust.
Is it better to remain forever cool?
Or we could pretend that tongue's
desire is merely play, then the mind's eye
may be momentarily beguiled
by the sight of cats, red and green,
now grown and clawing
birds from the enchanted air.

The Gardener in Middle Age

Hours before I left
I was weeding
as if I needed
assurances of order,
before the journey
to youth's reunion;
I hacked the Spring's
reckless growth
from the veggie patch
such a proliferation
of nameless grasses
and delicate runners
like useless thoughts
idle impressions
threatening to choke.

I wanted to leave
things tidy for new planting
and growth
a clarity of dark soil
to be scattered with hope,

but when I returned
the bed was obscured
by summer's abundance
a self-seeded riot
beggared the senses
tempting surrender
to my revenant chaos.
Look forward, you said
clear for Autumn, prepare
a winter harvest.

The Politician Retires

The thing is, Norman, I can call you Norman
after all these years you've been driving me?
The thing is no outsider understands.
The press, the public, they're like spectators at the match,
none of them can play, but they call and bray
from touchlines; they don't know the game
the skills, the pressure, the nudge and elbow
off the ball, the responsibility. And of course
it's all for them — you get paid for playing,
sure, but it's the performance that counts
the way the 'papers report it, the photographs
the image of it all. That's half the battle.
More than half. The way they see you.
And the work, no one sees the work you have to do
to make the first team, Norman,
the party meetings where D-grade hacks
walk their egos through procedural niceties
or covering their shiny arses
want to amend all motions; how you have to
soothe and flatter, bully and fawn,
practice the strategic lie and wield truth
like a machete, cutting down fools.
Is it any wonder after this you want a few perks?
And I know you've been discreet, Norm,
I can call you Norm, can't I?
I mean the way you waited outside *Fantasies*

on those cold Thursdays after the sittings,
a man needs some comfort so far from home.
But they've got me now on a trumped-up charge
fiddling the travel so they say,
it's a nonsense of course,
a few extra days in Fiji on the firm
a bit of extracurricular in foreign affairs
if you take my meaning, but the bitch dobbed.
So here I am reported, sent off, taking an early bath,
but it's not like I'll have to go to court,
the pension should be alright and I'll have to spend
a bit to square away the wife — an own goal
so to speak — but she'll be right, mate.
Anyway, here we are, the airport —
watch me smile for the cameras.
All the best old son.
Here's fifty for your trouble.

Rules of Engagement

Always choose the poor of the earth
to bomb, machine gun and terrorise;
they are used to oppression
to be a refugee is their ambition.

Tell no one what you're doing.
Say, it is for freedom and democracy,
that's enough for them to know:
manipulate the media.

Let the home front suck the pap
of popular culture;
it encourages ignorance and indifference
to the other peoples of the world.

Never state your aims clearly.
You may be pressured to stop
the killing before you want to;
suggest that it might go on for some time.

Make sure there are no images
of the dead, dying or dismembered;
show computer graphics of explosions
explain our success.

When in doubt deploy the strategic lie,
use all the resources of language
to deceive; bury the truth tellers;
say God is on our side.

Neighbourhood Guide

Our end of the battleaxe
is the one with the roundabout
where the kids play.
I wish it would turn.
But there's no magic
in this crescent — my word it's safe,
though the couple next door
from the Sally' army
can be heard taking care
of their late arrival
in strident tones of terrible alarm:
if she doesn't watch her step
Joy'll catch a hiding.
Michael, when not praying,
sells vacuum cleaners
in concert with God.
Listening to his spiel
my head drifted to blues
our chat unplugged forever.

Other neighbours remain obscure
tho' Bazza who works for water
gives a wave as he sweeps
away his week-ends
keeping it all clean
at the end of the day,
he sometimes shares a stubbie
with a used car salesman
who keeps erratic hours —
I've never spoken to Don
though I kissed his wife
one New Year's Eve at midnight —
'Every one's too shy round here,' she said.
I agreed, slurping red.
As for the other blade and haft
it's unknown territory.
We sometimes hear dogs bark at night
two places are owned by soldiers
and there's the safe-house —
irregular guests at all hours
we think they must be spooks.

Once in a while
through a storm at 3 a.m.
I think I hear screaming
pierce the blow
like fragments of pure pain
weird, uncanny.
But that's it. We don't want to know
keep ourselves to ourselves,
count bright blessings of boredom,
and when we hear of famine
wrack and civil war,
our daily dose of mayhem and atrocity,
we know it couldn't happen here
post charity cheques to make sure
we're all working towards the same end
an embattled privacy:
all the world a leafy suburb.

For Amnesty

In the cell there are no windows.
It is a darkness beyond night;
the walls shit smeared with indignity
encroach to trap the writer's mind
who, wide-eyed, dreamt of a free people.
And now, with broken fingers
and no voice he thinks only
of crisp white sheets, cloth and paper,
to wrap and nurture, to sail and sally
into the civility of sunshine
and market squares alive
with the gossip and squabble
of community in light so bright
it squeezes the eyes to tears.

All Cock Red

On the day the twin towers fell
I was teaching Greek tragedy
to a bunch of military cadets,
women mostly, 'Could you
explain *Hubris*,' they said.
C'est bizarre n'est ce pas?
Earlier that day we'd heard a General
'Ladies and Gentlemen today
our world changed forever
we are on security alert code
Weathercock Amber.'
(I bullshit you not.)
And things did change:
money had to be saved.
We had academic downsizing
and security upgrading
got to wear photo i.d. that made
a lot feel more important than before.
There were wars of course
in Afghanistan, Iraq, we were bombing

for democracy and happy in the trade
of terrorist surveillance;
people were banged up without trial
some were tortured for a good cause
and had their photos taken in the process,
tens of thousands of civilians died.
Imagine the bereaved being comforted:
Never mind, your mother, daughter, lover, died
in the marketplace for democracy,
every time you mark your fragile cross
you'll remember them and hope
for good leaders like ours
who are great; we keep voting them in
over and over again, little men with big cigars.
And yes, you guessed, we no longer
teach Greek tragedy. Hollywood is in
and somewhere, someone
is building Twin Towers again.

Corruption

The scales are rusted,
the defeated sword lies obsolete
language is twisted
in a mouth of broken teeth
and crumbled promises.
An ordinary life of child and wife
recedes to unreality
while a video entitled *love*
melts through the body's
cigarette singed screams.

And the torturer wakes
to the glittering day
his windows wide
and through that elegant frame
drifts landscape like a watercolour.
It soothes his eyes, replenishes,
ready for another night of play
at his high and fiery art.

The Weddings of Narcissi

I

They are shaping each other
applying the bevelled edge
to knock off rough corners
fashion their ideal romance.
It is the work of many days
there are abrasions when
the material seems knotty
resistant and suggests a
form quite other than the one
desired. Cunning is needed
plane and sandpaper, a smoothing
over, or sometimes a more violent
approach, the cutting deeper
more pronounced to oust
the irritant trait,
or unfortunate feature.
Their making love
is a rubbing each other up
the right and wrong way
an erasure of possible differences
indicating a need to preserve
the appropriate image.
It is a way to make statues
and photographs of statues;

it is a way to cheat change.
And so they chisel each other
in successive diminutions
for thirty years until
the finished product is admired —
how alike they are,
how they'll never alter —
artists of a marriage they
have sculpted the perfect exchange.

II

They fall for an armature
the possibilities of a straight ideal
fashionably thin
then add the flesh of clay
wet and slippery
in sensuous mouldings
through rub and finger
palm and pressure
they make each other
roundly every night
smothering imperfection
with new invention
a plastering over
until fat

they grow
into each other's
perfect lover.
But it can't go on
the clay dries
is fixed and fired
and they are chained
to forms from which
there's no escape
though they might brush
each other up
with different colours
or attach some
metal plated armour
the growing days
are over, no further
transformations
will move beyond indifference
they have become
finished.

The Doisneau Affair
(for Ellen, my daughter)

How you keep losing that kiss.
Once, you asked me to buy it for you
a poster of the Doisneau photograph
those '50s lovers, a romance
of foreign tongues, declaring bliss
a public boast for all the world
to hang upon their lonely walls.

I tramped the shops but couldn't find it
half grateful, I confessed, but you
were adamant, you would find those lips
joined in Europe, Paris, of course,
on tour with your beloved boy, maybe
at the Hotel de Ville you announced
your milennium version to the passers-by.

But would it, could it, last the distance?
Somewhere in the gloomy North of England
travelling towards distant rendezvous
the triste was left behind on a train
as if to say you knew that passion
could not thrive in those strict climes
of family: all that snow.

But you rang Lost Property, found
the lovers and flew them home to Australia.
And your sunny lad survived the trip
but on a bus transporting the precious photo
to be laminated, you lost it once again.
Did you feel so lucky you'd leave a tip
for the old farts of Petersham?

Now, I'm told, at last you've found the kiss
serene, it will decorate your young apartment
a reminder of difficult history and courage
I envy as I say in my crabbed way always
will you be able to bear this stolen moment
the knowledge that says, how parting lips
might mouth regret, frame such careless loss.

Avuncular

(for Andy and Mates at no. 49.)
(The road of excess leads to the palace of wisdom)

The boys on Golgotha Road
are living it large with beers and women
football and verse. Why not?
The address is enough to make them feel
the pressure of the skull beneath the skin,
each cobblestone to the front door
reminds them of a death's head
as every day they tread the road of thieves
and crackpot saviours who trudge
towards redemption via the tortured flesh and mind.

It's best not to live too thin
in this scenario of exploding martyrs,
the world shaking with broken glass and bodies.
It would be easy to let the fears take hold
make Mr Prudence in a bow tie with Bible
or Professor Pinstripe with a brief case
full of insurance. At home, the modest slippers
hot milk and Agatha Christie,
wandering the deserts of whodunnit virtue,
find Monsieur Poirot on the trail of terrorists.

My advice: don't overdo it. The palace
of wisdom is surrounded by a graveyard,
and there's more ways than one
to the cross at the steep end of the street.
Avoid self-help manuals and the doctor's orders;
if anyone's going to do Rolling Stones
you might as well be the one, and when
you find emptiness, then move forward
get into some passion on another road
large enough to live on.

The Task

He begins to understand
abstract sculpture
those reclining figures
not quite finished
full of negative space.

Somehow he has become
one of these hollowed ones
a head, discernable legs
but where the feeling
guts should be, a blank.

If he stopped to pose
people would see straight
through him to flat horizons
the innocent blues
of summer sky: always noon.

Or another variation:
all the figure's there
torso, pathetic genitals
the shy exposure of calf and flanks
but where the head should be

a round O, an empty
helmet, the mind usurped
the whole controlled
by the other's gaze,
becoming a clown of zero.

So he dreams of the heroic she
who will complete him,
figuratively, mould
a renaissance man
make a presence felt.

But he wakes alone
to the vacant day, knowing
he has to find the art within
must struggle to begin
his awful task of clay.

The Ageing Pedagogue

Surrounded by books and records
he sits in a haze of smoke and dust.
In the bathroom damp is rising
pipes are organs that groan with rust.

We listen to the latest rock bands,
classical vinyl too sad,
he says his long collection is evidence
of a life gone bad.

Even the car, he jokes, leaks water
sponging pools from the passenger seat;
the rear light is gone he says,
singing the darkness of his retreat.

The eminent scholar believing nothing
is the proper creed to teach,
finds a knee trembler in the doorway
preferable to articulate speech.

Is this what ageing romance comes to
the stranded only son,
who boasts to erstwhile acolytes
he still weeps for his long-dead mum.

Re. The Psychopathology of Corporate Greed

Like the cat when the door is opened
he hesitates before moving
regrets loss of comfort, warmth
the ministrations of approximate home.

Tense and poised he moves beyond,
sniffing the heady air of morning
into the street with no boundaries
the stranger city of the darker self.

Here is the hunting moment,
here the haunting tooth and claw;
he toys with death to enter
the lawless communion of desire.

And in the dawn the late return
to the frowsy habits of the
familiar bed, the meals, the purring:
he pretends domesticated.

In the Net

To live without zing, zip, passion or romance,
to make a virtue from mealy-mouthed 'content'
to say, 'I'll live alone in this thin flat
and have the best of everything,
a five thousand dollar stereo and huge TV
the newest of new age kitchenettes
and all the Vogue etceteras';
to have this uncontaminated space
sans partner, children, pets or plants
and sit behind the screen of a p.c.
watching, listening as the world unfolds
its chipped and packaged horror
the latest war, another exhibition
the review of several pop-psych manuals
which leave you helping yourself
with cybersex, courting a kind
of purity, coasting through
just this side of death but still
grateful for the conditioned air
and all the messages that fill the day —
email tantrums and textual games —
the only risk that slight chance
that someone might mention passion
                              or romance.
But then you're protected by cyberspace
and all you've bought and fashioned
into this slick, hip carapace.

Balancing Act

(After a painting by Romola Templeman)

Welcome to the painter's circus of dreams;
Pierette smiling on love's high wire,
does not look down, she has no safety net,
her eyes are fixed on some future bliss:
balance without compromise, skill without risk
smiles beyond performance.

Meanwhile a man in red and white striped vest
is juggling spheres of anxiety
his mouth a gash of wrapt neurosis
as if to fumble might mean hungry children,
disgrace to wife, and to the audience
an evening without miracle.

And in bleak corners of these tented walls
lurk the subtle gargoyles of desire:
a lusty centaur threatens chaos
prancing Punch is hooded violence;
Ambition squats on the high trapeze and waits
to cavort with Envy in the downthrow of rivals.

And so our canvas nights and matinees
reveal the panoply of human strife
to make the skills we practice for ourselves
bring delight to others; not for applause,
but anxious that what's revealed to public eyes
will assuage those prompting jesters in the dark.

Ars Poetica

It doesn't take much
a nudge of knees
beneath a table
the brush of hands
that scented hair
to get in touch
with this rogue emotion
who soon becomes
a swaggering larrikin
on the streets of imagination
where he struts
his scornful stuff
until to boast
he hurls a brick
at my house of glass
where each pain is framed
neatly contained

where order
like a hothouse flower
has been maintained
until this brick
lands with a thump
the mischievous vandal
has run amok,
and all my careful
defensive blooms
are threatened by
that powerful dude
itching for sex
spreading cool vibes
my life exposed
a destabilised text.

Mining a Heritage

(i.m. Sybil Allert)

I only knew you as 'old' Australian
five generations out from Cornwall
the Cooper and Nankivell miners brought
their non-conformist picks and shovels
to hue and dig a future country which by
your father's time had hardened and depressed.
Anzac memories, English banks were little help
so your dad turned to the Baker's van
in the '30s, biting the stale bread
of legendary laconic on his starving round
tears were for the weak or defeated,
your mother with raw red arms from
the washboard repeated the words:
a watery mantra. And from her too
you learned the pursed-lip style
'like a cat's arse', the rude boys
from the pool hall said, though they
too were taught the prejudices of
soap and bleached decency: eros sterilised
desire made underground, dark copper.

And I can only write you now as myth
while hand-sewn floral prints fade
into a country past, wanting in my city way
to dodge the fearful bigots simple in excess,
but still fix your dying image firm,
that layered history, the gleaming seams
of women's courage and endurance: threads
I seek the grace to pick and to unpick.

Didn't we have a lovely day?

Fish and chips from the boatshed
doing the usual Hitchcock jokes
warn our friends not to feed the seagulls
until the feast is finished.

Salt and sauce on greasy fingers
the sea made flesh within our mouths
sparkling orange is drinking sunshine
each palate kissed with fizzy bliss.

But the blue and white striped table
has been scarred by a careful knife:
the painted gaiety of all our high days
succumbs to the cut of 'Nothing Lasts'.

We fling some scraps to shag and cormorant
yet leave with our scraps of memory —
such guarded leftovers, a taste of friendship
to fill our hungers, there's little else.

Depot Beach

We walk to the beach through a dream of trees
and docile kangaroos who lift
their faces to track us with wary eyes,
until we emerge into diamond light
and hear the waves slap and thunder
along the crescent shore.
We print the sand with our desire to stay,
collecting such usual treasure:
shells that speak of painted homes;
the claws of creatures that once scuttled
through rock pools of our sub-consciousness,
a lump of wood sea-carved
and sanded to abstract art,
the wing feather of some broken gull.
But more than these in memory is the
tiny silver fish no bigger than a fingernail
its eye socket made for a matching chain.
I held the ruined creature in my palm,
wanting to preserve it like a charm
on some crafty maker's bracelet.
But I knew to keep it was to see it rot
and learnt that part of wonder which is
its fading back and living
          in the performance of a dream.

Formula One

Your need to ask me why I do it means
you'll never understand whatever I might say
of risk or challenge but since you've paid,
I'll try my best to give the usual tour
through days of childhood boredom
watching my father's drudgery —
a minor clerk in an insurance firm
eight hours a day making sure of profit
putting a price to insecurity —
meanwhile, I yearned for heroes beyond grey suits
soldiers, airmen, sportsmen, rock stars
such images of glamorous control
became ambition for adoration, fame
noone would scorn me
as they scorned my forefathers
soon growling engines high octane fuel became
a necessary inhalation, narcotic
danger drove me beyond the mess of failed
emotions and brought with it the girls I never
thought to have, and sex, but then there was
the mornng after … recriminations beyond control
to drive on the edge is more reliable

lost in concentration, how exact
each swift reacting change of gear,
battling the wheel for the right line
through every corner no slide or drift
to lose precious seconds or you life.
Once I read that every artist dreams
of complete freedom. I have no need to dream.
I've been there beyond the sordid bounds
of work, the prisons of suburbia.
Oh yes, I know, they pay me well, it's
the sport of capital, I'm millionaire.
But I don't care, the track, the other drivers
provide the limits to test my skill
and in those heady moments of adrenalin
towards the flag, you know there's nothing left
to feel, whether first or last you know
you've raced, survived, there's nothing more.
And if I die in some Grand Prix — well then
why don't you write down this:
one day each of us will drive a fast car
and no insurance will be big enough.

Detective Story

First a defilement of shagpile;
the mess that bodies make
like wreckage of a bird the cat's brought in,
guts and blood and bone
tattered shreds of nature
against the antique furniture.
How foreign the corpse seems
interrupting the tea and cake
politeness of a suburban afternoon.
Then the usual suspects: that family member
who demanded far too much,
resented how little the deceased
had to give, the secrecy, the lies;
move outwards to the circle
of fellow workers, those jealous of success,
power seekers passed over for promotion,
secret writers of risqué novels.
Lastly, investigate the bureacrats
who were refused obeisance,
their brusque imperatives
of efficiency and utility challenged;
the dictates of corporate money
threatened with subversion.
The plot unravels with focus on detectives:
a babe with a taste for satin and karate

leads a muddled innocent buffoon
who's half in love with her.
They take wrong paths,
narrowly avoid falling into bed.
The deceased is largely forgotten,
dissected in the hands of forensic experts.
Few attend the funeral. The corpse
of poetry laid to rest: death by
seriousness. A ring of mourners
wearing glasses and last year's fashions
blow their noses and utter epitaphs
no one understands.
Meanwhile paperbacks are producing
detective Donna radically entwined
with Lesbia on a double bed,
while her sidekick is seduced by the victim's
mother — a religious maniac.
The slinking competitor watches through
binoculars, and sees the way towards
a movie script: all the ingredients
cheap and thrilling. The last scene
is of steam cleaners trying to
erase the carpet's indelible stain.

Christmas Future

Do-it-yourself, bring your own
a virtual smorgasbord in cyberspace
shepherds updated to your choice
of used-car salesmen, estate agents
or insurance brokers, while kings
are a futures trader bearing gold,
a new age funeral director dispensing myrrh,
and doling the frankincense
a spin doctor wise with media healing.
The star is flashing neon.
You can choose your Inn from
Holiday, Hyatt, Sheraton,
and the baby may be born
in the garage surrounded by
Porsches and Lamborghinis.
There are no creatures here
but plastic angels trumpet
a continuous CD of popular hits
Shop in the name of love
before the game is up
and you can order your
customized feast by email.
It's a crackerjack program
of participatory fun
and you may be absolutely
reassured that there'll be
no mention of pain,
much less of salvation.

Pierrot Socialises

See him at the dinner party
watch him don the mask
Mr Entertainment makes them laugh
he'll tell a tale or two:
the one about the Northern barber
flogging a wig with a sly wink
'You can do owt in this auld lad
go swimming, wear it in bed,'
or try this one for macabre fun
how his grandma gassed the budgie
because its feathers were falling out,
you see the theme develop
they all laugh, he mimes the antic,
a smile like a murderer someone said,
and yes, they're about nakedness
and terror, but no one guesses
about the debacle in the throes of passion
the beloved left holding a handful of hair
like a dead spaniel, the ardent lover
with Sellotape burning down his bald head,
nor did they ask how the old lady
lured that bird into a plastic bag
or stop to wonder did he die singing
to himself, 'who's a pretty boy then?'
in the oven's choking dark.

The Clown Insomniac

Awake at 4 a.m. glum Pierrot
thinks of death and why he encourages
the growth of tumours with the ingestion
of cigarettes and buckets of cheap wine.
Perhaps I'm a Sybarite he assays
but it seems more likely that
the pleasure is punishment
for undisciplined desire.

And all his efforts to be, as it were,
good, to believe in compassionate
ideologies, to shield others from pain
cannot stop his unbuttoning fantasy
in a frenzy of mutual breathlessness
to awake the wonder of new touch
allowing discovery. He considers
his youth perhaps not wild enough.

But Pierrot has learnt repression well.
He resides part time in hell.
Anxious for dawn he pleads for light
and finds this image of fifteen years:
the hand of his beloved, intimate
when first they met as he lit her
cigarette; love's promise
steadying the uncertain flame.

Just Friends

On a good day Pierrot can jest
risking coffee with a winsome girl
and in his mind (*toujours l'audace*)
treats her to 'ee thou art a gradely lass'.
It lends a romantic patina
as she lips her lamington and
coconut dusts the conversation
which doesn't go beyond the politest
gestures, and never will, he knows.

Bound by the rites of masquerade
to toe the line and never tell his love
(tha'll not get owt for nowt auld lad)
instead he begins research on the
dinkum literature of loss. It's bound,
he thinks, to give joy a keener edge.

Pierrot's Complaint

What is this yearning to be young again?
What incompletion sends his senses spinning
at the sight of lithe girls and their handsome boys?
He feels like a dying cliché, the mid-life crisis man,
a walking paunch, the bald who was never beautiful or bold
a timid lusting Prufrock without the clever lines.
He watches their easy touching and sadly aches
bewildered by the emptiness of the crowded Mall.
He is a lost child wandering, a spotted bumbling teenager
with no grace, an ageing clown playing it all for laughs,
who no longer recognises the face that hides
behind the painted, leering mask.

The Muse Advertises

Female, single, mid thirties, seeks poet
non-smoker, moderate drinker,
preferably vegetarian or that way inclined —
Bohemians can stay in Bohemia
flogging themselves with poverty;
all that macho stuff about meat
is vain as vegan purity.
But still I want a man and one who
hates metaphysical sludge
who does not believe that poems
are little miracles and knows that
words speak more than fancy absence.
No minimalists need apply.
Hai-ku bores me, like pawing skeletons.
Give me flesh and the sensual dance.
I am enamoured of adjective
and metaphor sparingly deployed;
riddles are for children,
boastful cleverness is boring.
Let him speak plainly but not forego
moments of lyrical loveliness.
He may tell me for instance
that my eyes are like green sea stones

my lips taste of the waves' salt
or my body sways with the swing
of the sea — all this without rebuke.
Yet a little vulgarity may also be apt.
On tongues fragrant with chardonnay
he could delight to shock with his
risky expletive, an invitation
to country pleasures defeating the boredom
of a bland afternoon.
And afterwards conversation.
His tendencies should be democratic.
Aristocrats go loopy with inbreeding;
they mumble to themselves, dribbling
arcane phrases while the world
speaks out its rich and babel dance.
Lastly, let him be unafraid
of gentleness, forego posturing
and write for the writing's sake
knowing fame is a thin bubble
easily burst, substance
beyond all that fiddle.
Let him die crying love
in my arms.

A Poet Replies

Dear Muse in trembling answer
to your ad let me begin
with discouraging news.
I've been known to smoke
and stagger drunk through the politest
parties. I've also eaten meat.
Rejections have rained upon me.
I keep them like stale confetti
stored in a box long after the
divorce has been finalised.
I stand accused of poetic language
not hip or streetwise enough;
or else I'm too straightforward,
slapdash, artless.
Then, there's the question of difficulty;
my metaphors are not ingenious enough
or entirely absent, I'm prolix,
prosey, puritanical, plain.
I'm either too bourgeois or else
too political, not concerned with
nationalism or too personal.
Still I persevere, try to be sociable.
Let others get hooked on complexity
remember the beauty of water
after a night of heady wine;
an intellectual binge still leaves
a raging thirst and hunger

like the loneliness of blank rooms
when the party's over.
So I like my poems aspiring to crystal
cut with clarity, capable of ringing
with a depth of water or of wine
as from each facet shines
a different, shifting light.

But how to advertise myself?
Let me try this seduction
a fantasy of shy silences
caressed by whisky
a gentle unbuttoning
slipping off your sexy woollen dress
until we lie speaking the body's verbs
lips wet waiting for tongues
to dance entwining language
with a kiss.

Dear muse you see I'm up for it —
let's invent each other beyond fashion
and find in that romance enough to keep
us from too terrible a fear of
the dark, the cold and loveless death.
If we could make this miracle work
one or two others occasionally
might read our verse.

High School Concert

After the rock band — hip kids
in flannel shirts, daggy jeans,
a sexy, slender, female singer —
such studied chic and thumping blues —
came the classical trio:
a fat boy bursting from his suit
did his best with podgy hands to help
two lumpish girls, bespectacled
plain, hunched and buttoned up;
one stroked a timid violin
as if it might undo her,
the other choked a whispering flute.
All three were out of tune.

Bach was broken at their hands,
music wept, parents shuffled,
while I braced this unlikely hope:
that one day they might find
in proper time, a transforming touch,
the key in which to play and praise
some rich, harmonious melody,
turning, opening to the beloved.

Six Sonnets from the Hotel Australia

I

Two days alone I need a word
and there are no more poems.
So much for another Romantic lie,
or maybe it's that Rilke's way
just isn't mine — all that suffering
eros denied for the epistolary
to hear the angels sing etc.
Or not as the case might be.
For myself, reduced to ogling barmaids,
sipping chic in bored hotels,
I rehearse my need of speech to strangers
but what in this hectic time would be
an original, sparkling line?
'Darls, d'ya like your sonnets rhymed?'

II

Chained in the age of sexual freedom
I'm watching a woman on a bar stool
she holds a man between her legs
her hands caress his bum
is this more fun for me than him?
I taste each new development
wonder who is really right,
(professors of humanity disagree)
how have I learnt this tyranny of sight
badly taught or just blue genes?
It's impossible not to look and lust,
trained to neither act nor paint
all I'm left with is this dubious gift
an appetite to watch and write.

III

The pub again. Today I've brought my work
though poetry, I'm told, is a dying art
I'm willing to keep giving it a go
eavesdropping for material to shore
against an early ruin (whenever death
is mentioned it's mine comes to the fore).
But the living's not rich in this bar room drama
Let me take you to dinner, let me talk
I'll show you things you've never thought
I know how to penetrate your ... heart.
This bloke needs a collected works
to rouse her from a coma — as Shankly said
of football, *It's not a matter of life and death,*
it's more important than that.

IV

Pop art and movies, mate
that's what it's all about,
the news is pulp fiction
pulp fiction, news, get it
we don't need this fucking
elitist wank old son, you're in
the wrong pub, wrong bloody
century mate, take off for
cyberspace, be an astronaut
but don't come in here
jerking off in a corner
while I'm on the mobile
marketing myself.
Get a fucking life!

V

Watching yuppies or kids in grunge
is like reviewing those blindingly
clever post-modern writings
all display in different voices
'G'day mate how ya puttin it in?'
'The moon is like the bottom
of an empty gin bottle.' 'No one
gives a shit about youth on the dole.'
'Shares, Samantha, I'm talking shares.'
'Show me an access point and
I'll spin you out on the world wide web.'
'Spider, darling, shut up and give me a snort.'
How difficult it is to stop this malaise,
to find connections or to praise.

VI

After another arid day
plodding a jungle of dense leaves
this dangerous oasis
where swarming creatures drink and feed.

Young men in suits with mobile phones
exercise with splendid mates
their alligator brains
hungry for a killing.

They cruise the pool
snapping up talent
all jaws and teeth and smashing tails
the weak are hoovered in.

At the edge, timidly, I watch and graze,
digesting enough for tomorrow's page.

Remembering Charlie Middlehurst

His name more like a butcher's
he was the English master,
irony his cleaver
wielded with slick precision
an artist at dismemberment.

'Egan,' he'd say, 'you read
like a boiled egg',
or 'Stop staring Agostini Dean,
that boy with the motorbike,
you look like a hen peering
through long grass',
or this levelled at my sulky
'don't know, sir': 'Caesar,
you often strike me as a boy
who's drunk deep in the wells
of philosophy, but in reality
you've only passsed round
the pop bottle.'

None of this records
his silent, private life
the childless marriage
wife bound for years
to a wheelchair
his only recreation
bowls, a few beers at the club.
Such were rumours at retirement.

No, what we remember is
a Queen's Head tie-pin
the way we used to follow him
and whistle *The Red Flag*,
he'd turn and give a wordless V.
And though he hated poetry
what he taught us was
a way of fitting word to gesture,
a sense of personal style, and
whether in attack or self-defence,
his personal motto:
how the simplest English is the best.
He also showed in life and art
how sometimes silence
yields the greater interest.

A Carouse

(For Syd Harrex on his 60th birthday)

Remember that first evening, Syd?
We set course with schooners in two bars
then tacked into the hills, found port
in a restaraunt, I think was Viennese,
though by now fog was descending
our conversation lost,
we gasped the breeze, drove on
weaving higher into praise, beyond mist,
to your cabin at Coromandel
(Jane was away on holiday)
where, astonished, I watched you broach
another bottle, or was it two?
Refuelled we found our islands met;
you read Dylan Thomas, we raged
against the night, rode the reckless
storm of language in giddy joy
until oblivion at 4 a.m.

But you were Captain of the drunken boat
ringing the startling bell, imperturbable,
urging breakfast on me at six
before casting-off once more.
Now, years later, your lesson on board,
I wish you grand sailing as the glass falls,
and in each new dawn, language,
bold and sharp as orange juice,
the jaded palate freshened
by this heady craft of verse.

Dirty Realism

(for Cath)

Grunge in Sydney
is the coming fashion
bright young things
scion of Woollahra lawyers
pen fervid titillations
drugs and violent sex
erotic as a pap smear
their heroines
dying of ecstasy
ten bucks a time.

Meanwhile in Liverpool
a single mum in a single flat
tries to feed her baby, shivering
at the thought of the rat
that scampers not only
through her dreams and wonders if
the cheque will last this week
and if she'll have enough to eat
and how to get a job and keep
her child close to her.
Strangely she has no time
and little energy to think of sex
much less to read or write
or wallow in excess.

The Poet as Raconteur

Old Jellyback, Jack-the-lad,
tell 'em what they want to hear
tales of furious fornication
all blokey banter, no tears.

A few schooners, lots of smokes
everyone is reassured,
you can still speak the people's lingo
join the majority of the ill at ease.

So clumsiness, pain and dumb aggression
are turned to rich account,
in drunken bonhomie you become
an upmarket version of a lager lout,

practise preying upon the weak
the easy art of profligate speech.

Of Paving and Wilderness

(For Rick Hosking)

'What's your country then?' you demand
as if you've learnt in the blackfellah way
to know yourself part of a dreaming land
you belong to *South* Australia
where salt bush fringes lonely sands
and eucalypt embroiders remains of glacier,
climbing with eagles in folds of the Ranges
fishing and camping, you find your sacred places,
you can name flora and fauna, their history,
and shape from all this a life, an identity.

But I'm astonished by all I do not know
and wonder what failure has meant that I see
tree as tree, flower as flower, bone as bone,
not caring to name each rich particularity.
Did the grey squares of my pavement games
breed a craving for this abstract map
a careful art and mindful pilgrimage,
knowing what may be lost by being trapped?
In dreams I'm forever at airports weighing
the cost — torn between staying and taking off.

One Summer

(for Nicholas and Gillian)

Here is the light of paradise,
the Hazards off Dolphin Sands
not quite defined, their purple outline
softened by citrus haze,
which plays along a nine-mile beach
where lovers swim naked and alone,
while in the distance a rowing boat
rocks to remind that in heaven
there is always time for fishermen.

Dawdling home to the beach house
a modern space of wood and glass
with music rising to the beams
a secular cathedral of the blessed
where we taste communion
in daily rituals of work and play
sipping each sundown's chardonnay
before supper and the sensual dark
when night hands touch each other into sleep.

But how to keep this idyll bright
beyond one summer's epiphany
and not allow the winter freeze
to turn white gold to lead?
Somehow we have to learn the constant love
that moves and changes with seasonal light,
know the hazards, clearly defined
will try to sink us in storms blown up by habit
boredom, drudgery; have faith
to navigate the frightening plunge
as swimmers gasp laughing through icy waves;
learn the art of dreaming right.

Paris Sabbath

Gloomy interiors on a Sunday afternoon,
we come to the Church of St Sulpice
by a side door, in December, a young man in black
slumps forward his head face down
rests on his arms against the chair in front,
like a child chastised at infant's school
motionless, a sculpture of despair.
By his feet a single suitcase, also black,
suggests some homeless journeying.

In the nave three men labour to make
a model Bethlehem with hills and houses
the sound of construction echoes in the vault
a hymn to artisans amid the prayerful.
An appropriate carpenter, long-haired, unshaven
is hammering the scaffolding
of miraculous birth, with graceful nails
he fashions stable and manger,
despite his knowledge of the wooden cross.

An alcove reveals Delacroix's Jacob
wrestling with an angel. The human figure
straining muscle and sinew, hand to hand
with unmoving power, they could be dancing
or grappling towards some sexual buzz
but perhaps the point's the same:
how the struggle for our better selves,
the quest for love beyond indulgence
is like striving against a tree with wings.

We exit by the same side door where
the young man immobile still sits
apparently oblivious to the making
and the made around him; his sins too great
his body seems to say, for art's redemption
the birth and death of Christ too far away
to offer hope, and the resurrection a fairytale
for the soft headed. For myself it was enough
to hear the hammer ringing like a bell

summoning us to do our human work,
see Jacob indefatigable in the dark
sweating so the lonely, lost, betrayed
if they lift their heads from their despair
might find something that says they are not alone.
I also souvenired for art an image
of the unredeemed, the life in a battered case
that sometime must have moved forward
into the budding light of cold Parisian streets.

Concerning the Lost

It was Seferis who said
that poems are all around us
it's the poet's task to recognise them.
I used to think I had such moments
of illumination. The time for instance
on the Paris Metro I heard a busker sing,
'Those were the days my friend'
in Russian, and no one paid him.
That, I thought, might become a verse.
Or the dark girl in the tram,
miming to the crowd how difficult it was
to choose the right chocolate from the bag.
Full lips round soft centres.
And afterwards the way she shined her shoes
with a paper handkerchief as if she wasn't
sweet and shiny enough. I was almost certain
I'd seen something that might have been …
But it's over now. I'm stumbling in deserts
where fear is flying without a map
and razor wire cuts across eyes that peer
towards the receding horizon, dreaming
of houses, streets and shops: a civic future.
I'm trying to imagine half a million Iraqi infants
dead. I can't see them. Their eyes are blind.
The sewn lips of refugee children
make silence becoming.

A Charged Glass

(for Sally)

'Chardy Darls' offering the bottle
always with irony, sharp and sexy
strong fruit flavours.

Now the cellular dismay
the chemistry is all blood,
the tapped vein
pumped prophylactic.

'I'm not always at my best'
you say to friends.
'We never have been,' they reply —
three women weeping on a couch.

I'm watching, with a hint of gooseberry,
sipping all the courage
you give us, soon, I'll be drunk
on you and there will be laughter.

Once I said I couldn't praise.
It isn't true. When I saw you
giggling in your kerchief after chemo
it made me want to sing,

and now, watching the tears of friends
again, I want to hymn
life well-lived, the vitality
of wine drinking, friendship, love,
the well-cured red.

PANDANUS BOOKS

Pandanus Books was established in 2001 within the Research School of Pacific and Asian Studies at The Australian National University. The Pandanus Books catalogue focuses on books relating to Asia and the Pacific. The publishing list includes not only scholarly texts relating to the region but also embraces biography, memoir, fiction and poetry.

Since its inception, Pandanus Books has developed into an editorially independent publishing enterprise with an imaginative list of titles, a reputation for high quality production values and an international marketing strategy which promotes sales to a worldwide readership.

SULLIVAN'S CREEK PUBLICATION SERIES

The Sullivan's Creek Publication Series is a developing initiative of Pandanus Books, seeking to explore Australian cultural issues, literary texts, biography and history through the publication of both emerging and established writers who address a global audience. Books selected within this series are still published and marketed under the Pandanus Books imprint.